SELLING YOUR FAMILY HOME

WHAT THEY **SHOULD** TEACH EVERYONE AT SCHOOL

WHAT THEY SHOULD TEACH EVERYONE AT SCHOOL

SELLING YOUR FAMILY HOME

Written by

The Avocado Property Partners

ISBN: 9798322399407

Imprint: Independently published by Amazon KDP.

Copyright 2024, Avocado Property Group Limited.

All views expressed in this book are those of the author and are not intended for use as a definitive guide. The Avocado Property Partners are authorised distributors of this book. This work (content and rights) is owned in full by Avocado Property Group Limited. No part of this publication may be reproduced or transmitted in any form whatsoever without the written permission of a named Director: hello@avocadopropertyagents.co.uk

This book was produced in collaboration with Write Business Results Limited. For more information on their business book and marketing services, please visit www.writebusinessresults.com or contact the team via info@writebusinessresults.com.

WRITE BUSINESS RESULTS

ACKNOWLEDGMENTS

Everyone at Avocado Property Partners would like to take this opportunity to thank all of our clients, especially the people who have supported our journey from the start and those who have recommended us ever since.

CONTENTS

Acknowledgments   I

Introduction   V

Section 1:   1
Questions to Ask Yourself Before Moving Home

Section 2:   9
Valuations and Choosing the Right Estate Agent

Section 3:   15
7 Golden Tips to Get Your Property Ready for Viewings

Section 4:   19
The Marketing Plan

Section 5:   27
Don't be a Statistic: Why Over 30% of Offers Agreed Don't Complete

Section 6:   33
What is a Reservation Agreement and Should You Use One?

Section 7:   35
Questions to Ask When You Receive an Offer

Section 8:   39
What Actually is "The Chain"?

Section 9:   43
When is the Right Time to Start Offering on Your Next Property?

Section 10:   47
Solicitor Jargon Explained

Section 11:   53
Conveyancing Jargon Explained

Section 12:   63
Estate Agency Jargon Explained

Section 13: 67

What to to if You're Not Getting Viewings

Section 14: 69

What to do if You're Getting Viewings
but No Offers

Conclusion 73

About the Author 77

INTRODUCTION

Moving home is one of the top three most stressful things to do in England. This, ladies and gents, is a disgrace to the estate agency industry. This book has been written as a guide to help people navigate the outdated maze that is the English property market.

Who are we to offer such advice you might ask?

Avocado Property Partners has been disrupting the property industry for all the right reasons. We're on a mission to revitalise the UK moving process, making moving home as exciting as it should be. Yes, we have won awards; but our commitment to the industry runs deeper than recognition. We are building a brand that our children will be proud of when they grow up.

The knowledge we are about to share with you isn't taught in schools or training courses. This is knowledge gained from decades of experience, helping tens of thousands of people move home year after year in all types of markets.

Section 1:

QUESTIONS TO ASK YOURSELF BEFORE MOVING HOME

Question 1:

Why do I want to move?

Everyone has their own reasons for moving house. For some it might be a desire for more space, for others it's a matter of location. Perhaps your family is growing, or it's time to downsize.

Whatever the reason, understanding that all important "why" will help to reduce hesitation when it comes to decision making. Also, by identifying the "non-negotiables" for your move, you're less likely to be manipulated by buyers, sellers, or estate agents throughout the process. Everyone thinks this will not happen to them. That is until faced with the panic of missing out on something you love, combined with the pressure of the chain below and agents that may bend the truth to get their sales commission.

It can become a minefield. Always remember your reason for moving and keep this at the forefront of your decision-making process.

Question 2:

Are my finances ready, set and good to go?

If only it was as simple as finding the perfect house, falling in love with it, and working backwards from there. Life, of course, is rarely that easy, and without careful budgeting we risk being disappointed.

At Avocado Property Partners, we start with your why. Following this, the next step is to move on to your financial budgeting. We operate on this principle: if the money doesn't match the purpose of the move, wait until it does.

Over the years we have seen many people buy a property they don't truly love. Often this happens because people become fixated on the idea of moving and settle for second best, due to time pressures or budget. We frequently see this situation ending up in multiple moves within just a few years. Whilst this is great for us as estate agents, it's not so good for you or the money you've wasted on stamp duty.

To avoid this, here are some questions to ask your mortgage adviser when you start diving into the financial planning:

- Do I have a redemption penalty on my current mortgage?
- What will my monthly payments likely be?
- Should I do a two, three or five-year fixed-rate mortgage?
- What loans/debt do I have, and how will this impact the mortgage?
- Are rates falling or climbing?

TIP 1:

Never hide anything from the first prep conversation with a mortgage adviser. If you have a CCJ, debt on a store card, an accidental missed payment or anything else that will be flagged; just tell them. It will bite you on the butt later on if you don't.

TIP 2:

Different banks and lenders take overtime, commission and bonuses at different rates of affordability. So if you are paid in any way other than a straight forward basic, it is important to discuss that too.

Question 3:

What are my best and worst case scenarios?

Before you go searching for that dream home, have a little look into what you can afford based on a great offer and a bad offer.

Pricing the sale of your home is vital. Everyone loves their own home, and sometimes this means pride can get in the way. Unfortunately, not every person on the road can have the biggest plot, or the ex-show home. So budget on achieving a lowball offer. Then, set an ideal target price to focus on with the estate agent.

The market changes all the time and it's good to have the financial bracket clear in your mind before going to the effort of marketing your property.

Don't let ego or pride get in the way of making the move to your dream home happen.

Question 4:

What are my timescale expectations?

Every sale and purchase is different. Yes there are average timescales, but nothing is fixed until the contracts are exchanged with a set completion date.

2023 national averages:

- 62 days for the average property to go from "for sale" to "under offer".
- 4.1 months for the average property to go from "under offer" to "completion".
- Over six months in total.[1]

As you can see from the 2023 data, you need to give yourself time – don't gamble on a last-minute move. Moving home can be incredibly stressful. Most of the process is in someone else's hands: solicitors, buyers, estate agents, banks and surveyors. Add a chain of houses to the mix and things can take a little longer than expected! So give yourself and your family time to play with.

---

1   Data From TwentyEA

Question 5:

Am I mentally prepared to check out emotionally from my own home?

Moving home is a very emotional thing to do. As the saying goes: "your home is your castle".

Your home may be the place that your first child was born, the location you got engaged, or a multitude of other memories. Buying a home is personal, and it's easy to take feedback from buyers in this way.

Consider how you'd feel if you heard potential buyers comment on your home:

"I didn't like the area."

"The kitchen was not to my taste."

"Too much work to do inside for our standard."

Viewing feedback like this as personal can be incredibly hurtful. This is why it is vital that you "check out" emotionally from the property you are trying to sell.

If you have children, it's easier to focus on the new house. Get them involved and excited to pick out their new bedrooms, or have a new garden to explore. For yourself, keep remembering your "why" behind the move. Think about how magical it will feel to receive the keys on completion day. And remember: others' opinions of your home are not personal.

Section 2:

VALUATIONS AND CHOOSING THE RIGHT ESTATE AGENT

Reviews paint a picture

Before you choose the right estate agent, it is well worth having a look on Google at the ten most recent reviews.

Facebook reviews can also be particularly telling. This is because there is an option on Facebook that allows businesses to switch off reviews. So if an agent has no reviews, you may want to wonder why.

Experience of the valuer

When you ask for a valuation from an agent, ask for a person who has at least three years working in that local marketplace. A cheeky chap in a sharp suit at the beginning of his career may be full of energy and enthusiasm, but ideally you'll want to work with someone who has more experience. There is a lot of value in talking to an agent with "time in the market".

Most agents are not RICS (Royal Institution of Chartered Surveyors) chartered surveyors, which means they are coming over solely to pitch for the business, and may not have the highest level of technical property and market knowledge. The price point is secondary to them

Valuations and Choosing the Right Estate Agent

– winning the business is priority number one. It's a shame, but it's just the way it is. Unless, of course, you have an Avocado Property Partners partner agent working with you. We stand out for a reason.

Websites tell a story

Here is a little industry secret for you: you can tell a lot about a company by the value they offer on their website.

If an estate agency's website is outdated, un-professional, or generic does this communicate that they really care about their clients? When on the hunt for a professional, caring and on-the-ball estate agency, look for:

- Jargon–busting, helpful content offering free, valuable advice.
- Clear company values.
- Involvement in charity work or the wider community.
- A dedicated and helpful FAQ page.

Pay attention to marketing

Estate agents do not sell houses. Their job is to market a property to draw in a buyer, and then consult on the transaction to ensure all parties are happy. So, the marketing plan is a key part of what you are paying them to do. Some things to consider are:

- Is there a marketing blueprint that clearly identifies the target buyer?
- Is there a social media plan?
- Are you going to be involved?
- Will the agent do paid advertising outside of the portals?

Questions to ask on your valuation

- Is that a marketing price, or an achievable price, you valued my property at?
- What is your marketing plan to show my home to the right target buyers?
- Who will be conducting the viewings in your team, and how experienced are they?
- Who will I/we be dealing with directly throughout the whole process?
- What do you think is the most likely reason the house won't sell?

Valuations and Choosing the Right Estate Agent

- What is the plan if the property doesn't sell?
- What is the most likely type of buyer to offer on my house?
- What do I need to have and/or do before the house goes on the market?
- Who do I need to get quotes from to help with the move?

Reminder: If you wouldn't trust this agent to hold a key and show people round your property while you're out; then don't use them.

Selling Your Family Home

Section 3:

7 GOLDEN TIPS TO GET YOUR PROPERTY READY FOR VIEWINGS

1. First impressions count. Make sure the front of the house is tidy, clean, de-weeded and dressed to impress.

2. Move out ten per cent. Grab two to four boxes and get packing! We say ten per cent because that is normally enough to remove a few things you don't really need that may be cluttering the space, and de-personalise a little too.

3. Marketing. Good marketing and a great video will bring you serious buyers that are in the mood to buy! Settle for nothing less than 10/10 marketing from your estate agent – or it could cost you thousands. You need buyers to turn up ready and excited to look around the property (see the next section for our guide to marketing).

4. Bed sheets. It may seem like a small thing, but the successful sale of your home is made up of lots of small decisions. And let's be honest, a bedroom looks good based on the bed (the centrepiece) and the little furnishings around it. A bed normally takes up 75 per cent of the room in most bedrooms. If the bed sheets are

not looking clean and fresh, then people will be put off.

5. Clean! Bathrooms, toilets and kitchens especially, all need to have a hotel room feel about them. The white should be white, and the grout should be looking fresh. It will be worth the time and investment.

6. Something as simple as a lit candle in the hallway can make a big difference. Again, it's all about those little things that contribute to the overall impression. Food, pets and other smells that you may have gone nose-blind to, can be enough to put off potential buyers. A nice scent upon entry sets the tone – like a kid walking into a sweet shop! It just works.

7. To paint or not to paint! We advise looking in detail at high-traffic areas such as the hallways, stairs and landing. If they are well-loved, for example in families with young children, we would normally advise a touch-up.

> **WARNING:** Most estate agents just want to get your house on the market ASAP. They are not always the best people to take advice on this subject. (But any Avocado Partner is – we are a bit different ☺).

Section 4:

THE MARKETING PLAN

As we've discussed, buying a new property usually means selling your current home. Importantly, this sale needs to be at the right price point in order to make the finances work. To achieve this, your home needs a marketing plan.

This marketing plan needs to be bespoke to your home and your target buyer. The days of posting a property on Rightmove and picking a buyer seem to have passed. Unless, of course, you are happy to undersell your property!

Historically, estate agents have been lazy in keeping up with modern methods of marketing. For many, the extent of their marketing is to add a few nice photos and a floor plan on Rightmove, and then hope for the phone to ring. If their marketing plan does not go much beyond this, then they are simply not offering value for money in this day and age. Compared to the rest of the world, property marking in the UK is largely outdated and ineffective.

Solving a problem

Each home needs to stand out from the crowd. The marketing needs to show the unique key features of your house and paint a picture that shows potential buyers what it might feel like to live in the house.

Marketing a property is about talking to people that need a problem solved. For example, a buyer might need a bigger kitchen, to relocate close to their children's school, or an extra bathroom. The marketing plan for your property must show your potential buyer all the ways your house solves their problem for them. The video (if the agent does video) can't just be a selection of photos stitched together with some banal music. It needs to be engaging, presenter-led and emotionally moving to the buyer.

Reaching the right audience

The next part of a good marketing plan is showing the property to the right people. At Avocado Property Partners, we source more potential buyers for clients via social media than through platforms like Rightmove or Zoopla. This is not the "future of estate agency", it's the present. The more people that see your property marketing campaign, the better the chance of finding the right buyer at the right place. Times have changed, and now social media offers a fantastic way to achieve these numbers.

Exciting and engaging marketing showcased to a targeted buyer profile will be any seller's best chance of achieving their moving goals.

Don't settle for an average marketing plan. Make sure you have your say too – nobody knows your home better than you. Having your voice in the social media posts will build trust with the next owner of your home, which is something that a post filled with industry jargon will often fail to do (stay tuned for our jargon busting section later in the book).

TIP:

Before you pick an estate agent, check on their website and social pages to see how they market similar properties to yours online.

Don't risk being greedy when you launch

Most estate agents might say something along the lines of "you can only launch once."

At Avocado Property Partners, we know that's not 100 per cent true. We have a little trick up our sleeve that we use to test first. As we have a large social media following, we can do a test launch price, and a full launch price. The tester price is via our social channels and with the full video. We can even do a website landing page for the property, so people can check out the floorplan and pictures. As we don't launch this on Rightmove or Zoopla at this point, it means the ball is in your court when it comes to the "full launch" pricing strategy.

If there is zero interest in the social media launch, we can go for the full portal launch at "the right price", and if you decide to launch at a lower price than you tried with the test launch price via social media, it does not show your home as REDUCED on the portals.

In a climbing market, launching for a little more can sometimes work in the seller's favour. Even if you are slightly over market value in a climbing market, the chances are that pricing may catch up with you. Or, because of high demand, you might get lucky. In other markets, trying a little bit more than market value is a huge error. People scroll the internet for hours looking at property, and often way before they are ready to view. So if you out-price the market people will see it, and your home can quickly become "the one that's been on for ages". No property needs that tagline.

It is better to have the pick of buyers. Keep the ball in your court, pick the buyer that suits your price, your timescales and the one you like the feel of. There can be massive value in that process.

We call this: *creating a seller's market*.

Getting ready for photos and your bespoke property video.

Think: *colour and space.*

These are the two most important words to think about prior to the marketing work beginning. This is slightly different to getting ready for a viewing.

Space shows size and colour brings life, especially for the video. If you are marketing with an estate agent that provides a presenter-led vocal video then remember this is not a full viewing tour. It is a showcase video and, therefore, the two key rooms will likely get most of the screen time. This could also be said for the garden, so make sure that the grass is cut and there is colour in the flower borders if you can.

Flowers are great for the main rooms in the photos. You can see how your home might be viewed by potential buyers looking at photos and videos by taking a few test shots on your phone. Most smartphones these days are capable of producing high quality footage.

Here are a few extra things to think about before your home's big media day:

- Clutter
- Anything broken or damaged
- Cobwebs and dust
- Dirty windows

These are examples of little things that can go against you – and the camera doesn't miss a trick. You can photoshop an image, but a video is raw and authentic.

For Sale boards – yes or no?

Our advice on this is very simple: Tell the neighbours, and let's get cracking with full marketing.

Some people are not keen on "For Sale" boards and we understand that it can be a bit of an inconvenience. However, you just never know who has been waiting to see your house go up for sale. Even if you live in a cul-de-sac and you are right at the back, the board can help potential buyers find your home when they come for viewings.

This means the viewing starts on a positive note, rather than huge frustration because they can't easily identify which house they're looking for, due to unclear door numbers or low light.

Question to consider: If you are not ready for a board, might this mean that you are not emotionally ready to make the move?

#TeamForSaleBoard

Section 5:

DON'T BE A STATISTIC: WHY OVER 30% OF OFFERS AGREED DON'T COMPLETE

32 per cent is the national average in England for property sales that have been accepted, but do not complete. This is because either the buyer or the seller has withdrawn. There are hundreds of reasons why someone withdraws from a sale, but most of them can be avoided with the right team in place.

The most common reason property transactions don't complete is because the buyer changes their mind, or gets cold feet. This is the difference between the English and the Scottish property market. In Scotland the deal is done at the initial price agreed point, a little like an auction. In England a buyer can withdraw all the way up to the point of exchange.

In a fast-moving market for average price changes, a buyer could see a property like yours for £5,000, £10,000 or £20,000 less just ten weeks into the transaction of sale. As they have the option, they may decide to pull out of buying your property and choose another. What would you do? Not everyone withdraws and in fact most sales lose buyers in the first few weeks, coincidentally before the buyer has financially committed to a mortgage valuation (costing circa £350) and/or the property search pack (costing circa £300).

However, there is now a way to "take the buyer off market", just like you would take your property off market (more on this in the next section). There are some key questions an estate agent can ask a buyer to gain ultimate confidence. Some agents will rush to get a sold board up, while others will do the right due diligence. These questions are the difference between good agents and lazy agents.

Another reason sales don't complete, is surveys and mortgage valuations. Surveys can bring up unexpected problems. These problems will sometimes be compensated for, or in some cases the buyers are put off by them and walk away. On mortgage valuations (for and on behalf of the mortgage lender) there is a chance that the surveyor will down-value the property.

To down-value a property, as a surveyor, means they have researched other similar properties and the surveyor thinks the buyer is paying over the odds at the agreed price. They are effectively telling the mortgage lender not to lend the mortgage at that price and giving an alternative price. This sometimes means a re-negotiation on price, change of lender, or the buyer walking away from the sale.

Timing of the market will have a huge impact on the percentage of properties being down valued. In a declining property market, down valuations are more frequent. This is because surveyors are aware prices are dropping and, therefore, they must be more cautious in their pricing for the banks. In a climbing market, where prices are increasing rapidly, down valuations do still happen unfortunately. The truth is they often happen because the surveyors are not specialists in the local markets and are, therefore, unable to keep up with the pricing of recent sales.

The third and most frustrating reason people withdraw from sales are delays. Things taking too long cause people to become frustrated, and often they start looking elsewhere. One of the big problems when it comes to timescales is the conveyancing industry. It is a broken industry and if you go too cheap you will end up regretting it. The modern world is an impatient one. When it comes to house sales, the difference between exchanging and not exchanging in the agreed time can kill the sale. Some old school solicitors still ask for a fax number…

This is another area that a "good" estate agent can help sellers. Communication should start with the estate agent, and they should control the communication with each transaction. Legal work can only fully start when the agent sends the sales memorandums. From that point onwards everyone *should* be on the same page. Unfortunately, it doesn't always work that way.

On our website Advice Hub you can find lots of helpful and educational videos to try and prevent what we in the industry call "fall throughs".

Selling Your Family Home

Section 6:

WHAT IS A RESERVATION AGREEMENT AND SHOULD YOU USE ONE?

What is a reservation agreement you say? Fear not, this is new!

At Avocado Property Partners, we are partnered with a secure, Law Society approved, digital reservation agreement for sellers and buyers.

This works for second-hand property transactions in a similar way to what you would expect with a new home purchase. It's the only way in England that both seller and buyer will be "taken off market". Our expectation is that this will become "the new norm" inside the next few years.

Essentially a reservation agreement commits both the buyer and seller to a transaction. It means that transactions in England work more like those in Scotland.

If you want to know more about this, then please contact your local Avocado Property Partners agent on social media or via the website.

It's a GAME CHANGER!

Section 7:

QUESTIONS TO ASK WHEN YOU RECEIVE AN OFFER

1. Does the buyer have a property to sell?

2. Is it sold and how many links are in the chain? (anything over three links is likely too long).

3. Is the chain closed?

4. If they don't have a property to sell, what financial position are they in?

5. Are they currently renting? When is their tenancy ending?

6. Do they have any timescale needs or demands?

7. Is this the first (or only) property they have offered on?

8. What deposit to mortgage ratio are they buying with? (15 per cent deposit is about average).

9. What do they like about my property most?

10. Do they already have a solicitor ready to act?

Questions to Ask When You Receive an Offer

11. Do you trust them as a buyer?

12. If they are a cash buyer, where is the money coming from and will their solicitor confirm they have funds?

13. Do you have anyone else ready to view or is interested?

14. If the offer is agreed, will they enter a reservation agreement?

Selling Your Family Home

Section 8:

WHAT ACTUALLY IS "THE CHAIN"?

The chain in a property move are the links between properties that are connected by people. For example:

Imagine you are upsizing and your property has been sold to an investment buyer. You also have an offer agreed on a new home property. In this example, we have a chain of three people and two properties: yourself, the investment buyer, and the owners of the new home property. This is "The Chain", and in this example it is a closed chain.

The alternative to this example is an open chain from the top. This chain would have a buyer at the bottom who does not need to sell, buying your property, but you are still searching and so far you have not found a home. In this case, the chain would be open at the top because you don't have anywhere to move into. The same can happen if you then find a property to buy and agree an offer, but the sellers of that home are still searching. The chain is now one link longer and still open from the top.

When you are selling, you need to also be aware of an open chain below the buyer and what position this would put you in as a buyer. A buyer who is open chain below is also a seller of a property. They will be actively viewing and still

What Actually is "The Chain"?

searching for a buyer on their property at the same time. Sometimes these buyers will still offer on properties. However, this is what we call a "non-proceedable offer". If you accept their offer subject to them finding a buyer we would not advise you to take your home off the market for this buyer, as the chain is still open below.

The larger the chain, the more people that must agree to the terms and dates. This creates more risk for disagreements, obstacles and slower timeframes.

There are a few things to be aware of regarding chains:

First-time buyers at the bottom of the chain who are in rented properties will still have timescales. You will need to know about these and it will be based on the terms of the lease.

New build purchasing at the top of a chain will cause a timescale demand on the whole chain via the developer at the top. It is also important to know when the build completion date is set for the new build. Nobody can move into a house that has no roof... But! the developer will still demand the chain to exchange in a short space of time, often just four weeks.

Top of the chain is moving into rented space. Now this is not as simple as it sounds. Be aware that if the top of the chain plans to move into a rental property, then they will need to exchange *before* agreeing a rental. Timing this with a completion date is one step before impossible. So, this is really down to the estate agent to advise on taking a rental property prior to exchange (a gamble for the seller) or exchanging with the plan to stay with family while agreeing a rental property (also a gamble).

This happens a lot with people downsizing and the stress of selling, alongside finding a rental home they like (which is a fight in itself due to a shortage of rentals), can often blow the whole deal.

Solid advice and planning from day one is the key difference if this happens to become your chain.

Section 9:

WHEN IS THE RIGHT TIME TO START OFFERING ON YOUR NEXT PROPERTY?

Officially, you can offer on a home at any time. Even if you're not yet on the market, you can place an official offer "subject to selling". There is of course no reason that the seller will commit to you as a buyer with a property that is unsold, or take their house off the market while you are not proceedable.

Because of this, we would normally suggest offering after you have been put on the market and you are receiving viewings. This will also give you more of a power position when it comes to striking a bargain.

It is always a good idea to chat with your local Avocado Property Partners partner (if you're selling with us) as we can supply you with a 12-page bespoke data report on any property in the UK. This is one of the many perks of being an Avocado Property Partners client – it's great data too.

To find or to sell first – it's a bit like the chicken or the egg phrase. In truth the market dictates prices and any property that is "well priced" or "popular" is likely to sell quickest. This means if you are waiting for the dream house, other people are likely to be waiting for it too.

When is the Right Time?

The best advice we can give is to be proceedable (be ready) to avoid disappointment. If you are looking for something very specific that is unlikely to hit the market very often, we would advise working with a single agent on low-key marketing and an exclusive search plan.

Selling Your Family Home

Section 10:

SOLICITOR JARGON EXPLAINED

The legal process is broken into two main sections.

1. The money part

2. The conveyancing part

The money part is how someone finances the purchase of a property. Using either cash from savings, cash from sale, cash from asset sale or the most popular option, a mortgage.

If there is a mortgage involved, it is broken down into *four* sections.

First – A Mortgage Approved in Principle (AIP). This is when a mortgage lender does a micro check on a buyer and, without a property to proceed on, says, "in theory we will lend you the money".

Second – Mortgage Application. This is when a buyer has an AIP and now has an offer agreed on a property. The application is much more detailed and will flag up any issues.

Third – The Mortgage Valuation & Underwriting. The valuation is when the mortgage lenders check that they are happy with the property. The underwriting is the checks on the application.

These can happen in any order: valuation first, underwriting first, or at the same time.

Fourth – The Mortgage Offer! The final stage of the mortgage is the transaction before the money gets sent. Whoop whoop.

The conveyancing process is a complex one and can be very different for each property transaction. What is mind blowing is that the same property sale could be a totally different conveyancing experience from one solicitor to the next.

Solicitors like to work in the way (and speed) they like to work. Finding a good solicitor is like finding a good estate agent… Once you have one, stick with them for life!

Here are two lists that roughly show the order of play of an average property transaction.

AFTER SALES TABLE
(the money bit...)

Talk to your bank: always get a baseline from your bank first.

Talk to a good mortgage adviser: for a full market overview and vital advice.

Get a mortgage approved in principle: this is your AIP.

Find a property

Mortgage application submitted: this can't be done before you find a property.

Mortgage valuation paid: this normally happens using the card details you provided when you made your application – some banks do this for free. Note: this is not a full survey.

Mortgage valuation done: this can be a desktop (no visit needed), or a physical visit to the property by a surveyor.

Mortgage offered: sent to the buyer and solicitor.

AFTER SALES TABLE
(the legal bit.)

Offer agreed: full chain closed!

Solicitors instructed: for everyone.

Memos emailed: that means all legal parties are talking.

Draft contracts: these are sent by the vendor's solicitor.

Searches paid: paid for by the buyer and ordered by the buyer's solicitor.

Searches received: buyer's solicitor reviews.

Enquiries raised: by the buyer's solicitor and sent to the vendor's solicitor.

Enquiries reviewed: by the vendor and their solicitor.

Enquiries answered: answers sent to the buyer's solicitor.

Additional enquiries: new questions, often a bit of back and forth.

All enquiries answered: buyer's solicitor and vendor are happy.

Mortgage deed and proof of funds sent: by the buyer.

Agree completion date: buyer, seller and all of the chain agree.

Solicitor ready to report: final contracts sent.

All contracts back and dates agreed.

Exchange of contracts.

Completion!

Section 11:

CONVEYANCING JARGON EXPLAINED

Much like the House of Commons, solicitors have their own language. Hopefully this helps.

Completion date

One of the most exciting days you'll ever have, your completion date is the day where funds are transferred and keys change hands. Once the money has been exchanged between conveyancers, you've completed your sale or purchase and it's time to move in or out for good. If you're involved in a chain, all parties need to agree on completion dates, which is one of the reasons why chains can be complicated.

Contract

Also known as an "agreement for sale", your contract details the terms and conditions of the sale and purchase. This includes the price you've agreed and the completion date. When your conveyancer exchanges contracts with your buyer or seller, it becomes legally binding and you're obliged to complete the transaction.

Conveyancing

Conveyancing is the legal process which transfers the ownership of a property from one person to another. Your conveyancer will help you fill out all the legal forms required to process your sale or purchase, liaise with your mortgage lender and the other party's conveyancer, and complete tasks such as obtaining and checking the searches and transferring funds.

Deposit

Commonly, the amount of money needed on top of your mortgage to buy the house is known as the deposit. However, in conveyancing terms, the deposit under the contract will be ten per cent of the purchase price. Once you have exchanged contracts on a deal, you risk losing all of your deposit if you pull out. If you're buying and selling at the same time, your conveyancer will organise the transfer of your deposit from the funds you're receiving for selling your current property.

Disbursement

Disbursements are expenses that your conveyancer pays for as part of your move. This can include things like the costs of searches, and fees for registering details with the Land Registry. Usually, you will need to pay an up-front fee to your conveyancer, which covers the disbursements that are going to crop up.

Equity

The equity in your home is the amount that you actually own, as opposed to owing money to your mortgage lender. So, if your property is worth £200,000 and you have £75,000 outstanding on the mortgage, you own £125,000 of the equity in your home.

Freehold

When you buy a freehold property, this means that you have complete ownership of the land and everything built on it. This effectively lasts forever, until you sell the property. Subject to legal and planning conditions, you have the right to do whatever you want to your land and home.

Gazumped

Despite the lovely ring this word has, it's not a nice thing if it happens to you. Gazumping is where a seller accepts your initial offer, then goes on to accept a higher offer from someone else. As well as the disappointment, you can incur costs if you are gazumped, which is why it's important to stipulate that a property is taken off the market as a condition of your offer.

Land Registry

The Land Registry is a government department which maintains a record of properties in England and Wales. The register holds details such as when a property was last sold and for how much, keeping a record of titles on freehold and leasehold land and properties.

Leasehold

If the property you buy is *leasehold*, this means that the land your home is built on is owned by someone else. So effectively, you're buying the right to own a property temporarily, because another party ultimately owns the land. You'll likely have to pay ground rent to this person, and service charges can be payable if, for example, you buy a leasehold property in an apartment block.

Mortgage deed

This is a written contract which shows that you agree to a lender's terms and conditions. It also grants your mortgage provider a right in the property you are buying, as although your house will be your own, your lender can repossess and sell it if you don't keep up your mortgage repayments. This is why it is very important to be sure that you can afford the monthly payments, taking into account any potential rises in the mortgage rate.

Mortgage Agreement in Principle

Also known as pre-approval, securing a mortgage in principle from a lender means that you can get ahead of the game when it comes to house hunting. You'll know your budget, show sellers that you're a serious buyer, and be able to convert it into a concrete mortgage offer when you have an offer accepted on a property.

Mortgage offer

A formal mortgage offer from a lender will set out all the terms and conditions of your prospective mortgage. This includes details of the size of the loan to the mortgage product you're going for and your monthly repayments. Your conveyancer will receive a copy of the offer which they can go over and check the fine print on your behalf.

Redemption statement

If you want to amend or cancel your mortgage, or if you decide to switch providers, you'll require a redemption statement. Your existing lender will detail exactly how much of your mortgage is outstanding, and outline any early repayment charges or penalties. These are known as redemption fees.

Searches

As part of the conveyancing process, your conveyancer will carry out searches on the property you're buying. Searches highlight any potential issues which may affect your desire to purchase the property, and can include things like a local authority search, and water and drainage search.

Stamp Duty

Stamp Duty Land Tax is a government tax that's charged on property transactions. The tax is charged to the buyer not the seller. Some buyers don't pay any tax. The amount is calculated based on how many properties you own and the price you are buying at.

Surveys

To check your property is priced correctly, your mortgage provider will carry out a basic valuation. This you will normally pay for and although it helps you check the pricing is correct; really it is for the lender to check they are happy with the price.

It's usually worth carrying out an additional RICS survey which focuses on the state of the building you're buying. This can safeguard you from missing any potential problems with the structural integrity of the property, which could lead to costly repairs further down the line. RICS chartered surveyors will offer three levels of survey, starting with the basic Home Condition Report. The HomeBuyer Report is more in depth, while the Building Survey provides the most detail on your new home. The older the property the more in depth the survey should most likely be. Talk to The Survey Network (www.survey-network.co.uk) to discuss what type of survey you might need.

Title

When you have the title on a property, this recognises that you are the legal owner. The document proves your ownership, and while in the past your mortgage lender would have looked after the title in the form of original Deeds, these days the Land Registry stores it electronically.

Transfer deed

This is the document which officially finalises a sale, transferring the title of the property from the seller to the buyer. You usually sign this at the same time as your contract documents, and it'll be sent to the Land Registry so the property's title can be transferred into the buyer's name.

Selling Your Family Home

Section 12:

ESTATE AGENCY JARGON EXPLAINED

(Warning, this might make you chuckle)

"Lot's of Potential"
= Very dated, needs refurbishment and a strong chance it could become a money pit.

"Close to commuter links"
= Could be a motorway in your back garden.

"Low maintenance garden"
= Think concrete.

"OIEO"
= Offers in excess of, which 99.9 per cent of the time doesn't apply.

"Cash From Sale"
= Somebody that needs to sell their own property before they have the funds to buy yours; not a cash buyer.

"Gas cooker point & space for fridge freezer"
= No cooker and no fridge.

"Wood Effect"
= It's not wood.

"Viewings Recommended"
= They need a viewing to stay instructed by the seller.

Estate Agency Jargon Explained

"Realistically Priced"
− They overvalued it.

"Tenant in situ"
= There is a tenant in the property who probably doesn't want to leave.

"Part Furnished"
= The landlord left half their stuff in there when they moved out.

"The Chain"
= Nothing sinister here; the chain is the different property/people links that are involved in the transaction.

Selling Your Family Home

Section 13:

WHAT TO TO IF YOU'RE NOT GETTING VIEWINGS

If you are not getting viewings, it comes down to three main issues:

1. The Marketing

2. The Price

3. The Estate Agent

Questions you need to reflect on and ask yourself are:

1. How does my property compare to others online via the marketing? Include sold properties in your research too. Be honest with yourself and review your pricing vs other listings on the market. Sometimes this is good to do with a direct friend rather than just yourself.

2. Do I think my agent is doing everything they can? For example, are they taking seasonal photos? Are there strong, enticing bullet points in my property description? Is there a great marketing video? Have I seen social media posts and shares of my property to local Facebook groups?

Section 14:

WHAT TO DO IF YOU'RE GETTING VIEWINGS BUT NO OFFERS

If you are getting viewings, but not offers, then the issue is likely down to the marketing. Either the marketing is not selling the property as it should, or it is overselling it and causing disappointment. Either way, it's still worth reviewing.

A question to consider: *is the agent doing the viewings?*

The reason it's important to consider this is because it is essential that the agent knows enough about the property to sell its unique features. This is hugely important when it comes to the viewing experience of the potential buyer, as it could create a potential sale.

A second question to consider is, are the potential buyers who are viewing the property being qualified correctly or are they just carpet treaders? You can tell this via the feedback you are given from the estate agent.

Viewing feedback is important, of course, but here comes a whistleblowing moment... Unfortunately, estate agents in the UK have been known to fabricate viewing feedback. This is a tactic to help drive a seller's price down. So, if all the feedback you are getting is "They found one cheaper" or "They thought the price was too high", then maybe it is time to change agents.

What to do if You're Getting Viewings but No Offers

Finally, it might be time to accept that the price is not right and people are offering elsewhere after looking at multiple properties.

Selling Your Family Home

CONCLUSION

The house

Keep it clean, keep it clutter-free and keep in mind it is a transaction. Nothing is personal – remember the ultimate goal and try to be as unbiased as you can about your own home.

The timing

Seasons have an impact. If your garden is your top selling feature, it's probably unwise to sell in the winter. Sunshine makes everything look better! If you are planning a move for schools and need the move done before September, then give yourself a solid 9–10 months at least.

August and December are typically the quietest months of the year for buyer levels.

The professionals

Pick the people you pay wisely. If you use the cheapest solicitor, cheapest estate agent and cheapest removal company, then expect a few nightmares and a lot of headaches. If it sounds like a good cheap deal, chances are it will bite you in the butt when you really don't want it to!

QR CODE

We hope you have found this home moving guide helpful. Years of knowledge and time has been put into it to help the UK public.

At Avocado Property Partners, we are always updating the public on our social media channels. Feel free to follow us and don't be scared to comment on any of our posts too, we'd love to connect with you.

Conclusion

"We believe in the magic of moving home."

- *Everyone at Avocado*

Selling Your Family Home

ABOUT THE AUTHOR

The team of partner agents at Avocado Property Partners are all self-employed estate agents. Most of us have children, and got fed up with working in an industry with such a poor reputation. So together we are working to change it and build businesses our children can be genuinely proud of.

Founders Ian Macbeth and Mike Robson started the business six days before the first lockdown in 2020 – a strange time to start an estate agency business. However, the public in our local area totally embraced the change we offered. We went from suits and ties, to pink hoodies. From departments, to single contact with a business owner. Each agent is not just part of their community, they are in the thick of the community helping charities and local schools year after year.

We would like to say we have already made more than a dent in our industry, but we are far from finished and are happy to help and talk to anyone who wants property advice.

We hope you have taken some value from this book, and if you know someone else on the move soon it would be amazing if you share it with them.

The more people we can help the better.

Printed in Great Britain
by Amazon